Kingdom Files:

Who Was Jonah?

D1534623

Kingdom Files:

Who Was Jonah?

Matt Koceich

BARBOUR BOOKS
An Imprint of Barbour Publishing, Inc.

Print ISBN 978-1-68322-630-7

eBook Editions:
Adobe Digital Edition (.epub) 978-1-68322-898-1
Kindle and MobiPocket Edition (.prc) 978-1-68322-904-9

Cover design by C. B. Canga
Interior illustration by Jon Davis

Published by Barbour Books, an imprint of Barbour Publishing, Inc., 1810 Barbour Drive, Uhrichsville, Ohio 44683, www.barbourbooks.com

Our mission is to inspire the world with the life-changing message of the Bible.

Member of the
Evangelical Christian
Publishers Association

Printed in the United States of America.

06136 0718 CM

Dear Reading Detective,

Welcome to Kingdom Files! You're now a very important part of the Kingdom Files investigation—a series of really cool biographies all found in the Bible. Each case you investigate focuses on an important Bible character and is separated into three sections to make your time fun and interesting. First, you'll find the **Fact File**, which contains key information about a specific Bible character whom God called to do big things for His kingdom. Next, you'll read through an **Action File** that lays out Bible events showing the character in action. And finally, the **Power File** is where you'll find valuable information and memory verses to help you see how God is working in your life too. Along the way, **Clue Boxes** will offer applications to help you keep track of your thoughts as you make your way through the files. You can also use these sections to record questions you might have along Jonah's journey. Write down any questions, and then ask your parents to get them involved in your quest.

Before you begin, know this: not only did God have plans for the Bible characters you'll read about in the Kingdom Files, but Jeremiah 29:11 says that God has big plans for you too! I pray that *Kingdom Files: Who Was Jonah?* helps you get a bigger picture of God, and that you will see just how much He loves you!

Blessings,

M.K.

Name: **JONAH**
Occupation: **prophet**
From: **Gath-Hepher**
(just north of Nazareth)
Years Active: **786–746 BC**

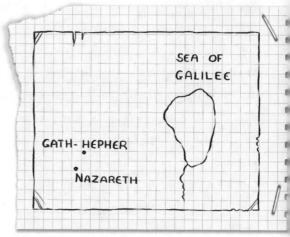

Kingdom Work: **preached to the people of Nineveh**

Mini Timeline:

793 BC
JONAH
BECOMES
A PROPHET

785 BC
JONAH
PREACHES
TO NINEVEH

753 BC
JONAH'S
MINISTRY
ENDS

Key Stats:
+ Called to share
  the gospel with
  his greatest
  enemy

+ Knew God was
  merciful and
  loving

+ Worshipped God
  through prayer

Run Away!

God had a very important job for Jonah. He wanted him to be a prophet. A prophet was a person God used to go and tell people important news about His kingdom. This was a very important job because it helped people turn away from selfish living and come back to a strong relationship with God. In many cases, the prophets had to go into uncomfortable situations to let people know they were making bad choices. They had to stand up for God, even when everyone else lost sight of what was truly important.

God talked to Jonah about a very special plan He had for his life. When Jonah heard the plan, he wasn't too happy. Here's why. . .

There was a really big city called Nineveh (almost five hundred miles away from Israel), and God asked Jonah to go there. The people who lived in Nineveh were not making good choices. In fact, the Bible says that the city was filled with wickedness. Also, Nineveh was the capital city of Assyria, the great and evil empire that was the enemy of Jonah's people. (Would *you* want to go into that city?)

Jonah didn't like God's plan because it meant that he would have to leave his comfort zone and trust God with everything. He didn't want to go to Nineveh, and he really didn't want to tell people what they were doing wrong. So guess what Jonah did? That's right, he ran away! It seems crazy that even though God personally called Jonah to do a big kingdom job, Jonah didn't want any part of it. But after gathering all the facts, we will see that Jonah was human and had many different emotions and concerns. Let's see how God worked in Jonah's life so that we can see the bigger picture of God's love and mercy and how those characteristics change lives.

∽∽∽∽∽∽∽∽∽∽

Jonah was the son of a man named Amittai, which means "my truth." Jonah was going to receive a very big job that had everything to do with sharing God's truth.

God wanted Jonah to share His truth in a city called Nineveh. That was one tough place, and Jonah didn't want any part of it. The people there lived life however they wanted and didn't care about God. Nineveh was also a great and powerful city. It was actually the largest city in the world during Jonah's day. That's pretty intimidating.

It didn't matter how wicked the city was, and it didn't mean a whole lot to Jonah that the people there heard the Good News. As far as he was concerned, they didn't deserve to be blessed. Punishment for their bad behavior was what Jonah was hoping for. He didn't want to bother going all that way to some crazy, faraway place just to be ignored.

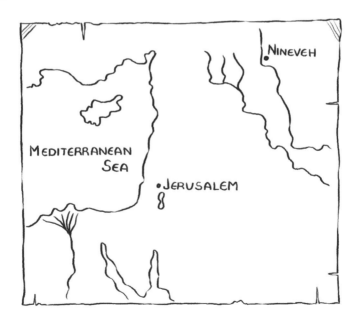

The first thing Jonah did was run away. Not just run across town. Jonah wanted as much distance between himself and Nineveh as possible. Across the sea was a port town called Tarshish.

That's exactly where Jonah decided to go. It would get him far away from the bad people so he wouldn't have to deal with the stress of it all.

Jonah had money and used it to buy a ticket for a boat ride that would take him to a distant place that was on the other side of the map from

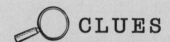 **CLUES**

Today in our world, there are people who look different and act different than we as believers act. They use bad language and listen to inappropriate songs on the radio and don't care about watching bad shows on TV. They don't believe in God and may even say that Jesus was just a good man but not the world's Savior. As we read Jonah's case, we need to pay attention to how God sees these kinds of people. We need to watch how God wants us to treat them.

Nineveh. Think about it: God saw Jonah and called him to do a great thing. Jonah knew God was faithful, and he knew how God had taken care of His people in the past. Still, something in Jonah's heart made him panic. He was trusting in what his eyes saw instead of the mighty power of God.

The Bible uses the word *flee* to describe Jonah's actions. He wanted to run the opposite direction from where God was telling him to go. He wanted to hop on a boat and sail across the ocean so he could "flee from the LORD" (1:3).

Jonah hopped aboard a ship that was setting sail for the faraway port called Tarshish. (And this is where Jonah's journey gets interesting.) God sent a great wind over the sea that Jonah's boat was on. The wind blew and grew, twisted and turned, until it became a violent storm.

The storm raged, and the boat was wildly tossed back and forth as the waves crashed, ready to break the boat into pieces. The crew panicked and started throwing their precious cargo overboard, trying to make the ship lighter in hopes that they could save themselves. The cargo was what they would normally sell to make money. But here in the middle of the furious storm, none of that mattered!

As the crew tossed their material possessions

overboard, the men were also calling out to their own gods for help. The strange thing is that the wicked storm didn't seem to bother Jonah! The Bible says that while the tempest (that's a razzle-dazzle word for "bad storm") was raging, he made his way below deck and found

CLUES

This is where Jonah gets his literal and spiritual wake-up call. If you're familiar with Jonah's story, you know a colossal fish was looming deep within the sea below. But this scene with the ship's captain demands your attention to the details.

Remember back at the beginning of our investigation, when we discovered that God was calling Jonah to go to the great city of Nineveh? There was a king in the city (we'll learn more about him later) who would eventually hear Jonah's message about God. If Jonah had obeyed God the first time, he'd have been standing inside the massive city walls, possibly speaking with a king; but instead, Jonah ended up inside the tiny wooden walls of a boat during a storm, while being yelled at by a ship's captain!

Poor Jonah.

a nice place to lie down. Can you imagine? A wild hurricane of sorts is spinning around your boat. Grown men are screaming, fearing for their lives. (What would *you* do?)

Well, while all that craziness was going on, Jonah fell asleep. And not just a light take-a-nap sleep. Jonah fell into a "deep sleep" (1:5).

But Jonah couldn't run away any longer. The ship's leader got right to the point. He yelled at Jonah to wake up. He then commanded Jonah to call upon God so that all of them could be saved.

Who's Responsible?

Meanwhile, the sailors were back on deck, still trying to figure out who or what was responsible for causing the violent storm. This had to have been the worst storm the sailors had ever seen, because they first tried dumping their precious cargo overboard. That didn't work, so they resorted to a time-honored method for finding answers: casting lots.

"Lots" were either sticks with markings on them or a handful of small, flat stones with symbols on each one. They were tossed into a small area and then interpreted. That's what casting lots meant back in the Bible times.

The men on the boat had to do something, and they had to do it quickly. So the sailors cast lots to see who was responsible for their bad situation. After the stones were tossed onto the deck, "the lot fell on Jonah" (1:7).

The Bible records Jonah trying to avoid the truth even at this point of his story. It was bad enough that he had run away from God the first time. Now, here he was in the middle of the tempest, jeopardizing not only his life but the lives of all the crew, running away from reality. Just like when he had tried to sleep away his problems, Jonah would try and talk his way out of this difficult situation.

The men asked Jonah whose fault gave rise to the storm. They asked him what kind of work he did. They asked him where he came from. "What is your country? Who are your people?" Did Jonah just stand there in silence? It seems so, because he didn't answer at first. He waited until after the men pounded him with their interrogation. And the response Jonah finally gave only answered one of their questions. "I am a Hebrew and I worship the Lord, the God of heaven, who made the sea and the dry land" (1:9).

It sounds like Jonah was telling the men that the storm was God's doing, which we already know is true. As a prophet, it was Jonah's job to stick up for God. Telling the sailors who the real God was helped get things back on track. But doing so came at a price. The sailors were terrified. They immediately asked Jonah what he did wrong to cause all this chaos. The Bible says that Jonah had already told them that he was running away from God. One way or another, the truth comes out. At least Jonah stood up for God sooner rather than later. And at least he stopped running.

But the storm raged on. Just because Jonah told the men about God didn't mean the stressful things in his life were going to suddenly disappear.

As Jonah would learn, things happen according to God's timeline. Jonah had tried to run ahead of God, but instead he would learn about the blessings that come from waiting on God.

The crew got right to the point and asked Jonah what they should do with him. They knew that somehow Jonah and the storm were connected. And since Jonah had made up his mind to stop running from God, he came up with an extreme solution: "Pick me up and throw me into the sea. . . and it will become calm. I know that it is my fault that this great storm has come upon you" (1:12).

Instead of saying he was sorry, Jonah went right for a drastic plan of action.

As it turns out, the sailors responded in an unexpected way. Instead of throwing Jonah over the railing like he was a piece of the cargo, they ignored his request and tried to row the boat back to land. They didn't react in anger. They didn't hurl insults at Jonah and blame him for their nerve-racking situation. The men simply put all their energy into coming up with a peaceful solution to a very difficult problem.

Imagine if you were on that boat. Would you want to be far away from Jonah? The men rowed, but the sea grew "even wilder than before" (1:13). This is where Jonah's disobedience was used for God's glory. Despite how bad the situation looked, inside the hearts of the sailors, wonderful salvation was on its way. They cried out to the one true God! They finally understood how things

should be. They had made a decision to honor Jonah's original request, but they wanted to make sure their hearts were right with God. They didn't want to harm Jonah, but they knew he didn't stand a chance once he landed in the water.

So what happened next?

The sea became calm. Peace covered the water, and the angry waves disappeared. Jonah was drowning, but the sailors were in a place they had never been before. They had just escaped a storm that had been raging in their hearts. The Bible says that they now "greatly feared the LORD, and they offered a sacrifice to the LORD and made vows to him" (1:16).

❧❧❧❧❧❧❧❧

We need to pause and think about all the clues we've gathered in our study so far. God invited

Jonah to preach the Good News to the people of Nineveh. Jonah said "no way" and took off running. The cool thing is that while all that was going on, the sailors were going about their daily routines, getting ready to set sail for another day's journey. They had no idea that a prophet of God was headed in their direction. They had no idea that the worst storm they'd live through was about to rise up.

The Monster Fish!

Long before the sailors tossed Jonah into the sea, God was preparing an escape plan for His prophet. Way back in the beginning of time, God was creating the world. In the book of Genesis, we read that God created the "great creatures of the sea" (1:21).

Jesus referred to a huge fish in the gospel of Matthew (12:40). God provided a monster fish to rescue His child. And just like Jesus was in the tomb for three days, so too was Jonah in the belly of the sea creature.

What would you do if you were Jonah? Panic? Sleep? Wonder? Maybe Jonah did all these things, but the Bible doesn't tell us for certain. What it does tell us, though, is that Jonah prayed! We see that Jonah was finally in a place where he could no longer run. He couldn't hide from God. The only thing he had left to do was pour out his heart to his Maker.

What did Jonah say to God? Here in the middle of nowhere—in the middle of the watery depths—Jonah first cried out to God, and God listened. Jonah's story tells us that in the center of his troubles, God provided answers.

There isn't some faraway place where we are beyond God's reach. Jonah said in his prayer that once he hit the water, he went down into the "realm of the dead" (2:2). But a great clue is found here among the words of the prophet's prayer: even though it looked like Jonah's fate was sealed, even though he felt like he was dying, the prophet grabbed on to the hope that

only God can give. Jonah reached out his hands and held on to the One who called his name. The One who is worthy of praise. Again, Jonah said that God listened to him. And what a relief it must have been for Jonah to know, without a doubt, that the God of the universe was there for him!

Real, gritty prayers—those are the kind of prayers Jonah was praying. He admitted that God was the One who threw him into the water,

CLUES

Can't you hear the praise rising up to heaven? Jonah is saying, *"God, oh wonderful God. You could have had me tossed overboard close to shore, but then I would have been able to swim back to safety by my own strength. If that happened, then I wouldn't be here now giving You all the glory!"*

but he didn't blame God or complain about his situation.

Jonah didn't miss a detail. He mentioned the strong currents swirling around him and said God's waves and breakers crashed over him.

It seems that Jonah had treaded water for quite a while (trying to save himself!) but eventually gave in and allowed himself to be pulled under. And then we get a glimpse of the worst part of Jonah's experience: "I have been banished from your sight" (2:4). Not the sailors. Not the storm. Not even the massive sea monster that swallowed him whole. Scariest for Jonah was actually believing that wherever he was, God had taken His eyes off of him.

At Jonah's lowest point, God must have reassured him, because he had an immediate change of heart: "Yet I will look again toward your holy temple" (2:4). What a memorable moment in Jonah's life as he went from the darkness of despair into the glorious light of God's promises!

Praying Hard

Sometimes it takes very difficult circumstances to make prayer something more than a checklist item. Praying not because you just feel like you want to, but crying out to God because you *must*. Jonah was in the belly of the great fish, talking to God about

his terrifying predicament. The prophet had tried to outrun his Creator only to find himself trapped in an ocean of bad decisions and life-changing consequences.

Jonah admitted that for a moment he thought life was over due to the deep ocean water surrounding him. "Seaweed was wrapped around my head" (2:5). Nature was preparing the prophet for a burial at sea. Jonah had sunk down to the darkest depths of the ocean. And there was an enemy lurking in the watery shadows. We know he was there. . .whispering to Jonah that God had surely abandoned him.

Down and down Jonah went until he couldn't sink any deeper. He wrote that he had sunk so far down, he had reached the "roots of the mountains" (2:6). As these events unfolded, it surely seemed that Jonah had run out of options.

But at this point in Jonah's tragedy, God

reached down and saved him. Jonah continued to give God all the credit by reminding us that it was God alone who brought his life up from the pit (2:6). He was telling God all the bad things that He had rescued Jonah from. And Jonah certainly didn't deserve to be rescued. He was the one who had run away from the plans God had for his life. Jonah was the one who had said no to the things God had in store for him. Jonah added that all he had to do, while in the belly of the fish, was think about God and pray.

Jonah also confirmed that God hears our prayers. He said that when his life was fading fast, God heard his cries for help. While his body was sinking, Jonah's prayers were going up to heaven.

CLUES

No matter what you're going through, your heavenly Father sees you and accepts your prayers. That should be as comforting to us today as it was to Jonah.

The prophet also gave a warning to avoid following after things of this world. He reminded us that if we grab on to stuff (worthless idols) in order to make us feel happy, we are turning away from the  love God has for us. Jonah worshipped himself when he made the decision to run away from God. He thought it would be safer to flee, and so he poured all of himself into that plan. He worshipped the idea of being in charge of his life.

But Jonah found something that had been hidden in his heart, and it was a wonderful discovery. He found the desire to praise God. He decided to worship God with "shouts of grateful praise" (2:9). This special statement proclaimed his true heart change. Jonah raised his voice so that his praise would be heard by many. At that moment, he committed to being a promise keeper. He vowed to tell anyone who would listen that "salvation comes from the Lord" (2:9). After Jonah came to this life-changing conclusion, God commanded the fish to spit Jonah out onto the beach. Then and there, the prophet could get back to the job God was calling him to.

5

On to Nineveh

Jonah had escaped death and was feeling really great. He was a changed man—a man alive and renewed. A man who wasn't interested in running away but instead wanted more than anything to do the things God asked him to do. Jonah wanted to give his life away to do the kingdom work that God had ready for him to do. No more self-worship. No more fear. Jonah was ready to listen to and obey the Lord.

God continued to be faithful. He never left Jonah alone in his disobedience. God forgave him and then provided a second chance for Jonah to be a part of the work He was about to do in Nineveh.

Jonah stood on the shore, free from the burdens of fear and worry. Restored physically and

spiritually to the One who called him to do great
things. And so, this is where God called back to
Jonah, "Go to the great city of Nineveh" (3:2). Even

though this was the
second time God told
Jonah to go, there
was no confusion
in Jonah's mind.
He was ready to go. He
was ready to obey. He
was ready to align his
heart with God's and

feel the peace that comes from a heart full of hope.

Finally, Jonah made his way to Nineveh. Nothing is recorded in the Bible about the journey he had from where he was on the shore to the great city. But we do know that Jonah desired to get there and start speaking truth to the people of Nineveh.

When Jonah arrived, he was overwhelmed by the sheer size of the city. The Bible said it took a person three whole days to walk through all of Nineveh. Jonah covered as much of the city as he could in one day. Along the way, he told anyone who would listen that their treasured city was going to be overthrown in a little over a month.

God gave the prophet courage and boldness to do the job he called Jonah to do. Jonah gives us a powerful picture of faith as he spoke words that were not easy or pleasant to speak. He didn't speak words that the people wanted to hear, and there must have been people there who heard what Jonah was saying and thought he was completely out of his mind.

Whenever God is involved, things don't always go the way the world thinks they should. In fact, after Jonah walked across one-third of the huge city proclaiming disturbing news, the Bible says that the "Ninevites believed God" (3:5). And they just didn't *say* they believed. They *showed* they believed by declaring a fast. That wasn't all. The people put on coarse, black cloth to show that they were mourning. The Bible says that "all of them, from the greatest to the least, put on sackcloth" (3:5).

Jonah got to see the results of his work.

Everywhere, the people of the great city were saying they were sorry and repenting. Hearts were changing, and Jonah witnessed it all. God was being glorified by the same people, who, only hours before, had no idea of the gift they were about to receive.

The King's Response

Imagine you are the great king of Nineveh. Your people are talking. They tell you that a foreign man is walking through your city talking about disaster coming your way soon. Imagine them telling you that everyone in your city is listening to this prophet and even going so far as to put on

dirty sackcloth and seek forgiveness. This behavior is unheard of in your land.

What would you do? See the man as a threat and have him arrested? Tell him he's crazy and have him thrown into prison? Remember, you're in charge, and you don't want the people getting weird ideas. It might cause people to question your authority, and you're the king! You definitely don't want that to happen.

The king of Nineveh did something much different. When he heard the message Jonah was preaching in his city, the king also responded in humility. He too, like his people before him, shed his royal robes and exchanged them for sackcloth. He didn't even wait until Jonah was brought into his palace. And when he was all done humbling himself before God and the world, the king took the final step of humility and sat down in the dirt!

The king's actions said that what God had to say was more important than his comfort.

The people of Nineveh had already humbled themselves after hearing Jonah's message. And even though the Bible doesn't give details, the

messenger who delivered the news to the king might have added a word or two about the people's reactions. The king probably heard that his whole city was on its knees, repenting before the God of the Israelites.

Either way, the important thing is that the king's transformation was all about his heart. The king wasn't just doing what his people did. The Bible says that he had been sitting on his throne when the news about Jonah came to him. And the hard, dirty ground became

the king's new command post.

From that lowly position, the king issued a new decree. He said that he didn't want any person or animal to eat or drink. Then he added the command that all people and animals should be covered in sackcloth! Even the animals! (Can you believe that?)

And the king didn't stop there. He commanded everyone in the city to "call urgently on God" (3:8). He said that everyone needed to stop acting ugly and hurting each other. The leader was telling the people that they needed to do business with the only true God. The king had spoken. His response was an act of love for his people because God had stirred his heart to seek forgiveness and restoration.

The king's heart was turned toward God's. He was beginning to understand the attributes of the Father. He said in his decree that he knew God had a compassionate heart and that his hope was in Him.

A new rain of salvation washed over the land. True freedom was on its way to the people of Nineveh. After everything they did to make themselves humble, the Bible says that God saw their actions. It says that God watched as the people "turned from their evil ways" (3:10). Most of all, God held back and didn't bring the destruction that was set to fall over them.

The whole city had heard the Good News. It was time to celebrate, but Jonah was anything but happy!

7

Jonah's Anger

An unbelievable thing had happened. The biggest and meanest city in the land humbled themselves and received God's forgiveness! The great city of Nineveh had turned from its bad choices and decided to follow God. But as they were celebrating, the prophet Jonah was quite upset!

It doesn't make sense, does it? Jonah had just had an amazing transformation inside the fish. He had prayed an amazing prayer about how God had saved him and how good life is when you turn to God's love.

But for some reason, it wasn't enough to keep Jonah's emotions together. Maybe he was exhausted from all the traveling and preaching. Whatever it was, Jonah became angry. He felt it was wrong that all the people of Nineveh had sought forgiveness.

Even though his behavior is opposite of what someone might expect, Jonah prayed. He didn't run away again. He talked to God about how he was feeling. He told God that it was the reason he ran away. Jonah said that he wanted to run away to "forestall," or prevent, this outcome. Jonah knew God's will was best. He knew that his actions weren't going to change the hearts of a nation. That it was all up to God.

Jonah was just being honest and open. He couldn't believe the city that once did its own thing was now praising and praying to Jonah's God. It just didn't feel right to the prophet. So, in his confusion and emotional distress, Jonah decided to list some of God's many attributes. It was all he could do to make things work out with waves of

conflicting feelings crashing over his soul.

Jonah started off by saying that God was gracious. Jonah knew that above all, his heavenly Father was the ultimate grace giver. Jonah had just experienced that grace in back-to-back scenarios: first with the fish and then in the miraculous conversion of Nineveh. Even though Jonah was mentally exhausted, he wanted to speak the truth: God is full of grace.

Jonah also said that compassion is another one of God's important attributes. God cares about His people. God's heart is for His children.

Next, Jonah said that God is slow to anger. Jonah was understanding that God is patient with us. God called Jonah to minister for His kingdom and glory, but Jonah ran away. God didn't get angry with Jonah. He pursued him, meaning God kept following Jonah and never left his side. God kept inviting Jonah to join Him and was there to rescue Jonah when he needed help.

And God is always abounding in love. Jonah knew that he served a God who doesn't love like humans do: God's heart overflows with love in an unending waterfall of mercy and desire.

Finally, God relented from sending calamity. God waited and held back. He is the God who seeks relationships, and Jonah also witnessed this in his brief time in Nineveh.

In another turn of emotions, Jonah asked the Lord to take him away. Jonah would rather have been with God in heaven than have to deal with all the emotions that came with the job of preaching in the big city.

God replied with a question: "Is it right for you to be angry?" (4:4). He wasn't going to turn His back on Jonah. He wouldn't leave Jonah alone because the prophet had an emotional breakdown. That's what the enemy wanted: division and separation.

The Bible doesn't include Jonah's response. All we know is that Jonah left the city and found a place to sit down somewhere to the east. He made a shelter for himself and rested in its shade. Jonah stayed there and "waited to see what would happen" to Nineveh (4:5).

8

God's Gift

Jonah's story has two parts: all the things Jonah decided to do for himself and then the things he did for God.

The wonderful ending is what God did for

the weary prophet. God didn't end the story by judging Jonah or getting mad at him. No, that is not how God operates. God doesn't condemn; He provides. "Then the LORD God provided a leafy plant and made it grow up over Jonah" (4:6). God saw the shelter Jonah had fashioned for himself and wanted to give His child more. And God not only gave Jonah better comfort in the moment, but continued to provide comfort for him.

God also wanted to ease Jonah's pain. He didn't want Jonah to worry or fear. He didn't want Jonah to go to some faraway land and suffer. God gave to Jonah, despite his disobedience and temper tantrums.

If Jonah's story were a Hollywood

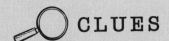

CLUES

Remember that God is gracious. He acts and blesses not because of what people do, but because of who He is.

movie, it would end here. There would be no more

investigation into Jonah's life. Jonah would live happily ever after. But God had a lesson for Jonah to learn. God wanted Jonah to become more and more like Him as he traveled life's journey (which is what God wants for all His children). So God "provided a worm, which chewed the plant so that it

withered" (4:7).

Jonah's shade was taken away, but God didn't stop there. God "provided a scorching east wind" (4:8). The elements became harsh, and Jonah began to feel faint. For the second time, Jonah responded to God by saying he was ready to die.

> **CLUES**
>
> God does give and He takes away, but He doesn't change who He is or how much He loves us.

God challenged Jonah again and asked if he should really be upset about the plant dying. And Jonah very directly said that he had every right to be angry and that he wished his life were over.

God responded in such a wonderful way. Jonah was about to hear that he had been looking at life through the wrong lens. God wanted His prophet to listen to what was really important in life. God was about to tell Jonah that the most important lesson he needed to learn was that people matter. And not only that people matter, but that their hearts are not something to ignore or walk away from after a brief interaction. God wanted Jonah to see the permanence of living a life in relationship with all His children.

First, God reminded Jonah that he had done nothing with the plant. Jonah hadn't created it or taken care of it. The prophet had invested nothing, so he should not have been concerned with it.

Second, God was trying to show Jonah that people are more important than things. God wanted Jonah to focus on the fact that the people of Nineveh were so much more important than a plant.

Finally, God taught Jonah that He cares about all people, even those who are spiritually lost and, like children, "cannot tell their right hand from their left" (4:11).

This is where the story of Jonah comes to an

end. Now it's time in our investigation to see what lessons we can take away from Jonah's adventures.

9

POWER FILE

Jonah had a gritty, emotional, easy-to-understand story. As we finish our investigation of God's honest prophet, there are several lessons that God would have us take away from our time learning about Jonah's life. We are all called to spread God's truth. Jesus is the Way, the Truth, and the Life. If He is your Savior, then you are His child, and you too are also a son or daughter of Truth! As we looked at the Kingdom File on Jonah, we uncovered many clues that show just how much God cares for His children. And not only that, but we saw over and over again that God cares for all people. God wanted the people in Nineveh, who were really messing up their lives, to hear about His love and saving power. The story of Jonah also shows us that God never walks away from His children. He doesn't talk to us one minute and then take off the next. He is a loving Father who has great plans for us. Now, just like Jonah, sometimes we have a hard time believing what God says; but in the end, we are called to live a life of faith and believe that God's plans are the best. For example, God could have prevented Jonah from getting on the boat, but we saw that God used Jonah's life to reach even more than just the people of Nineveh. God waited for Jonah to get on the boat because the sailors on the boat needed to see truth too.

How comforting to know that God is always there for us. He hears us when we call on Him, and He provides ways out even on the darkest days.

Power-Up #1:

OBEY GOD.

God wants the best for His children. And part of our exploration of Jonah's story shows us that everything God says comes to pass. In one way or another, God's will is always done, and it's always for His glory. We have the opportunity and blessing to see Jonah's story from the vantage point of the finish line, looking back over the course of his journey. We can sit here and say, "If only Jonah had obeyed God the first time instead of running away to Tarshish!"

So, today take note of this important lesson to help you avoid having regrets. Don't get caught on the wrong end of the "What if?" question.

MEMORY VERSE: Love the LORD your God and keep his requirements, his decrees, his laws and his commands always.
Deuteronomy 11:1

Power-Up #2:

DON'T BE AFRAID.

When Jonah first heard of God's plan, he thought it was crazy. The prophet knew that Nineveh was filled with wickedness, and he didn't want any part of that city. On some level, the prophet was probably afraid. He must have temporarily forgotten that God was so much bigger than the great city that was the cause of Jonah's anxiety. We need to continue living each of our days praying and reading God's Word. And when we hear God speak a certain plan for our lives, we need to be fearlessly obedient!

MEMORY VERSE: "Be strong and courageous. Do not be afraid; do not be discouraged, for the LORD your God will be with you wherever you go." Joshua 1:9

Power-Up #3:

GOD CARES.

God cares about His children. He valued Jonah and saw worth in him. God wanted to use him to do big things for His kingdom. Yes, God knew Jonah was going to run away toward Tarshish, but the beautiful part of the story is that God didn't let Jonah go. God cared for His prophet by sending storms. The change in weather that, at first glance, seemed like a sinister punishment was really a gentle nudge to bring the prophet back on track.

God wanted to have a caring relationship with Jonah. And the way God was always there for Jonah is the exact same way God is here for us today!

MEMORY VERSE: You have searched me, Lord, and you know me. You know when I sit and when I rise; you perceive my thoughts from afar. You discern my going out and my lying down; you are familiar with all my ways. Before a word is on my tongue you, Lord, know it completely. You hem me in behind and before, and you lay your hand upon me. Psalm 139:1-5

Power-Up #4:

GOD LOVES.

The Maker of the universe doesn't need help, but He does choose to have His people be a part of His kingdom work. It didn't matter how Jonah reacted to his situations—God didn't change His plans because Jonah threw a fit. Instead, God continued to love Jonah despite the prophet's ever-changing moods. And God met Jonah with love on every step of his journey. From graciously listening to his prayers to providing for all his needs, God loved Jonah—and today He showers us with the same kind of love. It's a love that calls, fulfills, and best of all remains. This should inspire us to know that we too are filled with God's love as we live life with Him!

MEMORY VERSE: Whoever does not love does not know God, because God is love.
1 John 4:8

Power-Up #5:

GOD IS FAITHFUL.

Because we know that God is faithful, we also need to understand that He never leaves us alone. We have an enemy named Satan who tries to make us believe lies. God proves Himself faithful all the time. There isn't a moment when God loses control or steps off His throne. The Bible says that the enemy is a good deceiver and wants us to feel forgotten and unloved. But the Bible also says that Jesus died for every one of our mistakes because God loves us so much. This makes us feel better on those days when nothing seems to be going right.

MEMORY VERSE: God is faithful, who has called you into fellowship with his Son, Jesus Christ our Lord. 1 Corinthians 1:9

Power-Up #6:

LIVE BY FAITH.

If God is faithful, we need to live each day and each hour by faith—no matter how hard life may get. The fact that Jonah finally went to Nineveh despite originally wanting to run far away shows that he understood that living life while remaining anchored to God's will is the very best way to live. Imagine Jonah standing on the beach after the fish spit him out on the sand, taking a deep breath as he looked toward Nineveh. Maybe he said something like, "Okay, God. Thank You for saving me. I'm sorry I tried running away. I still don't feel like going to Nineveh, but now I'm ready to do things Your way." Maybe Jonah exhaled and took his first step toward the big, intimidating city. But still Jonah put all his faith in his God, who went before him.

MEMORY VERSE: I have been crucified with Christ and I no longer live, but Christ lives in me. The life I now live in the body, I live by faith in the Son of God, who loved me and gave himself for me. Galatians 2:20

Power-Up #7:
PRAY HARD.

Another big lesson we can learn from Jonah's story is that talking to God through prayer shouldn't always be simply asking God for things. God deserves more from us. Praying hard means that we also use our conversations with God to glorify His holy name as we tell Him what He's done for us. For example, instead of something like, *God, please help me not to feel scared*, we can change things up and pray, *God, You are*

Almighty. All throughout the Bible, You have
protected people and given them the courage
to be brave. Please help me not to feel scared.
Remember, the enemy doesn't want us to pray.
He would rather we disconnect from God and
do our own thing. Commit to praying hard
and staying connected to the One who loves
His people more than anything.

MEMORY VERSE: This is the confidence we
have in approaching God: that if we ask
anything according to his will, he hears us.
1 John 5:14

Power-Up #8:
GOD IS GRACE.

Oh, how blessed we are that God gives us grace instead of what we truly deserve. Jonah's story is overflowing with examples of God's grace given at all the right times. When Jonah took off running, God showed him grace by going after Jonah. When Jonah said no, God still showed him grace. When the storm came and threatened to sink the sailors' boat, Jonah used the opportunity to be honest with God.

As Jonah was being tossed in the sea, God was there to catch him in a wave of grace. The enemy is doing everything in his power to make us feel like we're one mistake away from God shaking His head and walking away from us. But this isn't truth. God is grace. Forever. And when we mess up, God is there to show us grace. Live your life full of thankfulness for everything God has done and is doing, because He is grace.

MEMORY VERSE: Let us then approach God's throne of grace with confidence, so that we may receive mercy and find grace to help us in our time of need. Hebrews 4:16

Power-Up #9:

GOD DOESN'T ABANDON.

What a comforting thought to know that God will never leave us alone. No matter what we are going through, God wants us to understand that He won't walk away from us. He doesn't change. Remember, the enemy wants us to believe that God doesn't care about us. Satan wants us to think that our unanswered prayers are proof that God has gone away and left us to figure things out on our own. But Jonah's story shows that what looked like God's abandonment—the storm, the giant fish, even Nineveh—was actually a blessing sent from God to provide a way for Jonah to become closer to his heavenly Father.

MEMORY VERSE: God has said, "Never will I leave you; never will I forsake you."
Hebrews 13:5

Power-Up #10:
GOD PROVIDES.

As we've seen many times in our investigation of Jonah's story, God is with His prophet at every turn, providing just what Jonah needs, just when he needs it. The Bible says many times that we shouldn't worry; and Jesus even tells us that we shouldn't worry, because He provides. First the storm, then the great fish, then the plant for shade—God gave Jonah just what he needed, right when he needed it. These three gifts were forms of protection, but God also provided purpose for Jonah. He called him to share the Good News with Nineveh, providing Jonah with a job that mattered in God's kingdom. God also provided opportunities for Jonah. The whole Nineveh experience gave Jonah a chance to be an important part of God's mission. Remember that God also gives us what we need when we need it. It may not seem like God is answering our prayers, but He will always provide for us in His time.

MEMORY VERSE: "But seek his kingdom, and these things will be given to you as well." Luke 12:31

Matt Koceich is a husband,
father, and public school teacher.
He and his family live in Texas.

Notes

_____

_____

_____

_____

_____

_____

_____

_____

_____

_____

_____

_____

_____

Notes

Notes

Notes

Collect Them All!

Kingdom Files: Who Is Jesus?

This biblically accurate biography explores the life of Jesus while drawing readers into a fascinating time and place as they learn about the One who gave sight to the blind, made the lame to walk, raised people from the dead, and who died so that we might live.

Paperback / 978-1-68322-626-0 / $4.99

Kingdom Files: Who Was Daniel?

This biblically accurate biography explores the life of Daniel while drawing readers into a fascinating time and place as they learn about the faithful man of God who interpreted dreams for the king and ultimately survived a den of hungry lions.

Paperback / 978-1-68322-627-7 / $4.99

Kingdom Files: Who Was David?

This biblically accurate biography explores the life of David while drawing readers into a fascinating time and place as they learn about the shepherd boy turned king who played a harp and slayed a giant with a stone and a sling.

Paperback / 978-1-68322-628-4 / $4.99

Kingdom Files: Who Was Esther?

This biblically accurate biography explores the life of Esther while drawing readers into a fascinating time and place as they learn about the beautiful Queen of Persia who hid her Jewish heritage from the king and ultimately risked her life to save her people.

Paperback / 978-1-68322-629-1 / $4.99

Kingdom Files: Who Was Mary, Mother of Jesus?

This biblically accurate biography explores the life of Mary while drawing readers into a fascinating time and place as they learn about the courageous young teenager who said "yes" to God and ultimately gave birth to the Savior of the world.

Paperback / 978-1-68322-631-4 / $4.99